how 2

Perfect

wedding/ceremony!

REVEREND SANDRA LYNCH

Owner of Ceremony Alchemy, formerly Weddings by Sandy

©2013, 2016 by Sandra Lynch
Printed in the United States of America

ISBN: 978-0-9914204-0-7

Contents

What is an Officiant?

An Officiant is someone who writes and/or reads ceremonies for couples getting married, presides over the wedding ceremony, and signs the legal documents. A great Officiant is someone who is a ceremonialist over the wedding ceremonies and doesn't just read the ceremony but rejoices with the couple, has a great speaking voice, and handles wedding-day issues calmly and with grace.

From meeting to ceremony

The following is an overview of what to expect when working with an Officiant –
from your first meeting to your ceremony and beyond.

Pre-Planning

Your first contact with an Officiant will most likely be through an email or a phone
call. The Officiant whom you requested or who is available will try to set up a date
and time to meet with you and your fiancé(e). Some of the most important information your Officiant will need to know is your wedding date, time, and location. Just
like other wedding vendors, Officiants book months in advance. The meeting is not
only to ascertain if you and the Officiant are a good match – for personality style and
level of expertise – but also to give the Officiant the opportunity to explain everything you need to know about working with them, how they handle their business,
how they solve problems, and what you can expect during your ceremony.

During your Meeting

Meeting your Officiant is a great way to learn more about what they have to offer.
Each Officiant comes from a different background, so meeting with them allows you

to get to know them a little better. Meetings might take place halfway between where you live and where the Officiant lives – in a coffee shop or restaurant, in your home, or in an office set up especially to meet couples. Schedule a date and time that works for everyone and give your Officiant a chance to meet you and to explain the fees, the contract, and other aspects of the ceremony.

Expect meetings to last around 1–1.5 hours in length. Allow yourself to be open with the Officiant when you meet; let your beliefs and values be known and tell the Officiant how you met. Explain what kind of ceremony you would like to have – what your vision is for your wedding. Your Officiant will show you sample wedding ceremonies and may offer you many other choices. Listen and then ask any questions you may have. You should be prepared to put down a deposit if you really like the Officiant.

After the Meeting

Do you still have questions? Contact the Officiant and ask your questions. They will be happy to assist you.

If you want to book your Officiant, don't hesitate. Most Officiants speak to lots of couples and don't solidify their schedule until they get a retainer and a contract.

You will want to get your license, at least, one week to one month before your wedding ceremony is scheduled. Make sure you follow the instructions given to you by your Officiant and the county authorities.

Once you decide what will be in your ceremony, make sure your selections get to your Officiant, so they get a chance for review, editing, and suggestions.

Meet with your Officiant as often as you deem necessary to complete your ceremony.

Rehearsal

Inform your Officiant of your scheduled rehearsal as soon as possible but not later than one month before the actual rehearsal date so that they can be sure to be available on the date you have selected. You may want to have a conversation about your rehearsal a day or two before to understand what is required and what to expect. Let's just say that the rehearsal is important for a perfect ceremony, especially when you have more than one or two people in your bridal party; at least then they know what to expect during the ceremony.

Ceremony

Most Officiants arrive at least 30 minutes before your ceremony; this way they have a chance to interact with the other vendors to ensure your ceremony is perfect. Typically, your Officiant will have a kit of problem-solving items with them to ensure everything goes off without a hitch. During your ceremony, a thoughtful Officiant will have tissues in their pocket and be very aware of what is happening around them and with you.

Following the Ceremony

Following the ceremony, your Officiant will sign your documents and take care of your license appropriately. A copy will be mailed to or dropped off at the correct county office. Your Officiant may ask to take photos, do a short video testimonial, or something similar. Your Officiant is there for you even after your wedding ceremony – if you have a problem with your license, want to have a baby naming for your new baby, or need funeral services for a loved one, just call and ask.

Why it is important to budget for a professional Officiant?

Most people think of their wedding ceremony as 15-20 minutes of necessary. Well, to me it is 15-20 minutes of pure heaven. Why? Because this is the best job I have ever had! I am a professional wedding Officiant, someone who cares about you and the words you say to each other on the most important day of your life! A professional Officiant is not just someone who strolls in 15 minutes before your wedding and then reads a nondescript, unmemorable ceremony that may or may not reflect you as a couple. Rather, a professional Officiant is someone who has spent a lot of time before the ceremony working with you, preparing the script to meet your wishes and dreams, and is eloquent, calm, pulled together, organized, a polished speaker, has a bag of tricks to help you on your wedding day, and much, much more.

So, when couples call and say, "How much do you charge?" Honestly, I want you to know there are more things to consider than just the cost. For example:

- Am I available?
- How much did you budget?

- How far do I have to travel?
- How much time do I need to invest?
- Do you have a large bridal party?
- Do you want a rehearsal?
- And of course, what level of service are you expecting or want?

Yes, of course, it is about you but first, it has to be about me, because I need to know exactly what you are looking for, asking for, and expecting. The wedding ceremony is the focus of your special day, and honestly, a wedding Officiant is the only vendor you actually need to get married. So, budgeting enough for this critical part of your wedding is very important.

According to Rev. Laura Cannon- Owner, Ceremony Officiants and President of the IAPWO, "First impressions are everything. The ceremony is your guests' first impression of your entire wedding day. The quality of the ceremony is not only determined by the quality of the words that are written, but by the skill in which they are delivered. When calculating your wedding budget, it's important to consider the value that each item has towards making your wedding day one to remember. Guests will remember a great ceremony far longer than an artisanal cheese plate (which often costs more!)"

According to the Wedding Report, in 2014 wedding Officiants cost averaged about $207 across the United States. However, you have to take into account that some Officiants, Ministers, and other faith leaders do not charge for their services.

According to Tia Paul, owner of Cashmere Events in Baltimore, Maryland, couples should budget a minimum of $300-$600 for their Officiant. Personally, I feel that couples who only budget enough for a courthouse wedding should go to the courthouse. Officiants are not county clerks who get paid by the county. Some are not associated with a church, unlike Ministers, Priests and Rabbis who get paid by their church or temple and may require as much as $300-$1000 for a donation to the church or temple to officiate a wedding. Some may require you to rent the church and provide a stipend. So, costs can vary a great deal.

Professional wedding Officiants are just that, professionals who have learned everything there is to know about weddings. They travel to your venue, customize your ceremony, attend rehearsals, some provide blessings at the rehearsal dinner and reception dinner and much, much, more. You may be their only source of income. Most Officiants are hardworking individuals who often have a family, hold down a full-time job or several part-time jobs to create a living and work as an Officiant on the weekends. Most full-time Officiants, cannot make enough

money on weddings to live on and as a necessity do other things such as funerals, baby namings and other creative or wedding oriented jobs. Just like you, they have mortgages and financial obligations to meet.

So, how much should you budget? I would say budget enough to get a great personalized ceremony, an Officiant, who understands your vision, who has a great personality and speaking voice. It also depends on what your area demands. On the east and west coasts, budgeting $600-$1800 is completely appropriate, because wedding Officiants are in great demand. You also have to figure out if there will be travel charges, rehearsal fees, costs for sounds systems, robes, food, and accommodations for your Officiant. In the central US, maybe $300 is enough. Look around; ask around.

The point is this: you get what you pay for. In the wedding industry, you can literally, buy anything, and people are willing to pay for what they want. But look at it this way; since the wedding ceremony is the core and purpose of your day, why would you skimp? Pay for a great, meaningful, authentic, personalized ceremony. You will be glad you did. Let a wonderful professional Officiant help you. You won't regret it, and you will have warm feelings about your wedding ceremony for the rest of your life.

Six things you need to know about professional Officiants

As a wedding officiant, I work with all kinds of couples looking for wedding ceremonies ranging from a 5-minute simple ceremony to a wonderfully personalized ceremony. Of course, my goal is to provide something meaningful, beautiful, appropriate in length and perfect for each couple.

So, with that in mind, here are the top six things you need to know about professional Officiants.

1. **Not all Officiants are equal. There are two kinds of Officiants. Amateurs and professionals.**

   Amateur Officiants are part-time, rarely get paid or charge very little, have zero training and do not take the officiant profession seriously, maybe just do it for fun, as a hobby.

   Professional Officiants are passionate about the couples they work with, love creating marvelous ceremonies, know how to speak in front of people and are serious about giving the couple an amazing experience.

2. **Professional Officiants charge too much!**

   Most of us rarely question our dentist or doctor, and they are professionals. I wouldn't want to risk my dental care with a dentist who was not thoroughly trained and didn't know what they were doing!

I feel the same way about my ceremony and the Officiant to choose. I want someone to charge me a fee and provide a contract to ensure they will be at the ceremony. Execute the ceremony as planned, understand how weddings work, have creative ideas, support me during the process and much more!

So how much is too much? In the Mid-Atlantic region, the median fee for professional Officiants is around $600. However, Officiants may charge anywhere from $500 to $1800. The range is significant because it depends on what you want.

How much time the Officiant has to give to the process and what kind of an Officiant they are will make a huge difference in pricing. For example, a non-denominational cantor sings the ceremony. This unique kind of Officiant is used mostly in Jewish weddings and demands more of the Officiant which will cost you more.

There may be additional fees too, such as travel, tolls, accommodations, rehearsal and more. I think, starting your budget around $500-$700 will get you a beautiful ceremony to remember for the rest of your lives.

3. How long will the ceremony last?

Most American wedding ceremonies average around 17-20 minutes; some are shorter; others like Catholic wedding ceremonies are longer. It depends on the setting, the time you have set aside, your expectations, your parents' expectations, and your officiant's hopes for a ceremony they can execute with style. Sitting down with your family and the Officiant to explain your vision is how you will get your wedding day needs, and expectations met.

4. How soon should I meet with and secure my Officiant?

Many couples meet with other vendors as far as 12-18 months in advance. I suggest at least nine months in advance. Once you secure your venue, book your Officiant. Why? Because our calendars fill up fast, just like other professional vendors; don't take a chance and lose your special date! Some dates are very popular, so booking in advance will ensure your special date gets you on your officiant's calendar.

5. Not all Officiants conduct rehearsal.

This is not uncommon, some officiants just don't consider rehearsal a necessary part of the process, because you can walk, right? Some may sit down and chat about the ceremony; others will come and do rehearsal as part of their package, and other will charge extra.

This difference is important for a couple of reasons. Some officiants love going over the parts of the ceremony so everyone understands their part to play, meet the parents and the attendants and make sure they can find the location on wedding day. It can be helpful, but weddings are often conducted without rehearsal every day, so it depends on the complexity of your wedding, you and your officiant's comfort level and the personal style of your officiant.

6. Finally, today's Officiants are more than just ministers.

Like other professionals, Officiants come from a variety of backgrounds. Some are public speakers, some are retired ministers, some were professional singers or actors, and others might have been

in the military. Ask your officiant why they do weddings ceremonies, you might be surprised to learn why they do what they do.

Enjoy the planning, the process, and your wedding ceremony more. Hire a Professional Officiant to help you make the centerpiece of your wedding day stand out.

Questions you may be asked during your first meeting.

Here is a short list of questions I typically ask during a meeting with a couple. I think these are just some of the things your Officiant might need to know to understand what you are looking for so they can create a meaningful, personalized,

and special wedding ceremony. It is best to be open and honest and allow your Officiant to get to know you so that the process will be easier for all of you.

1. Tell me how you met!

2. Are you religious, spiritual or non-religious? What is your religious background? Is religion important to you?

3. Regarding religion: Is there anything you do or do not want to include in the ceremony?

4. Describe your perfect Officiant.

5. Speaking: are you comfortable speaking in public or do you want to keep it to a minimum?

6. Writing: do you want to write vows to one another? If you wish to write your vows but not read them to each other, you can repeat after the Officiant.

7. Are you interested in any of the many rituals that can go on during

a wedding such as a sand ceremony, a rose exchange, wine sharing, candle lighting, or hand fasting?

8. Are you planning to use a runner? Please note: these don't work well on uneven surfaces such as grass or outside. Save your money and use rose petals instead; besides rose petals are prettier.

9. Are you including music such as a vocalist or music that will play while I am speaking? Please note: music and speaking don't go well together unless I use a microphone.

10. Is anyone doing a reading?

11. Describe your guests and your family. How many are planning to attend?

12. Have you worked out the processional? Will it include formal seating of parents and grandparents?

13. Describe your relationship – What do you think the key for you to live a long and happy life together will be?

Questions you should ask the Officiant

Is the Officiant available on your wedding date? Just like other wedding vendors, Officiants book months in advance.

Can the Officiant travel to your chosen wedding site? Is there an extra charge for mileage or airfare?

If you don't have a site for your wedding ceremony, can the Officiant suggest a site or provide one? Does the Officiant charge a "standard" fee? What is a standard fee? What types of things does this fee cover?

During your Meeting

Let your beliefs and values be known. Explain what kind of ceremony you would like to have. Look for an Officiant, who will treat the ceremony with the right amount of reverence.

Ask lots of questions, such as:

- Why does s/he perform weddings? Are the reasons consistent with your needs?

- Does the Officiant have sample vows, ceremonies, and readings to show you?

- Will the Officiant let you specify ceremony details such as music, readings, and vows?

- Is the Officiant willing to discuss non-traditional wedding ceremonies and traditions?

- Is the Officiant available for a ceremony rehearsal?

- Do we have final say over the script?

- How soon before the ceremony will you arrive?

- Does the fee include a full rehearsal?

- Do you require a retainer fee?

- Will you work with our other wedding professionals? How?

- Does it matter how many guests I have? Will that affect the fee?

- Will you be respectful to my family members?

- Is there anything else can you tell us about your services?

After the Meeting

Are you comfortable upon meeting the Officiant?

Does s/he seem genuinely interested in you as a couple and is s/he willing to assist you with the creation of the vows and ceremony you've always wanted?

Would you like the Officiant (and his/her spouse) to come to the reception and rehearsal dinner?

Officiant hiring tips

OFFICIANT HIRING TIP #1

Be certain the person you hire knows how to use a microphone if having amplified sound! You would be surprised to learn the number of wedding Officiants who do not know how to use a microphone.

OFFICIANT HIRING TIP #2

Make certain the person you hire offers an acceptable backup, in the event of their sudden unavailability. The loss of voice, illness, a death in the family, etc., is possible. Life situations should not leave you stranded on your wedding day!

OFFICIANT HIRING TIP #3

Make certain that you will have a say in the type of clothing the Officiant will wear to your ceremony. A simple black suit is better than hot pink unless that's what you wanted!

OFFICIANT HIRING TIP #4

You get what you pay for....I'm just saying! I cannot tell you the number of times I get a phone call from a panicked couple, whose Officiant has not shown up or who dropped out at the last minute.

A typical wedding ceremony consists of

Pre-Ceremony Music – Music for the guests to listen to, moms and parents to walk in to, and the groom and groomsmen to walk in to.

Processional Music – for bridesmaids and bride to walk in to Opening Words – Why are we here? Welcoming words Presentation of the Couple (optional)

Readings (usually one or two) (optional)
    Poetry can be anywhere in the ceremony

Prayer (optional) Address (optional)

Declaration or Expression of Intent (Optional)
    Questions to the bride and groom about their intentions to marry.

Words about the Vows

Marriage Vows

Blessing of or Words about the Rings

Exchange of the Rings – Make sure to tell your Officiant if you are not each exchanging a ring

Special (Optional) Ceremony such as Candle Light Ceremony or Rose
Ceremony

Pronouncement of Marriage Kiss

Closing Words – Final Benediction Presentation of the Couple (optional)
Recessional (Music)

How to have a more productive wedding rehearsal

Here is a list of tips and hints that may help you make the most of your rehearsal time. These tips are my opinion and based on real-life experiences from having performed hundreds of wedding ceremonies and rehearsals for many years. I hope you find it useful.

Purpose of the Wedding Rehearsal

The rehearsal is the last step in guaranteeing a stress-free wedding ceremony. Rehearsals are typically conducted the day before the ceremony and often are followed by a rehearsal dinner where the couple thanks their most trusted friends and family members for supporting them during this stressful time. The purpose of the rehearsal is to give everyone involved in the wedding the opportunity to figure out all the tiny logistical details of entering, exiting, which way to face, handling the rings, the bouquet, and any special rituals being done during the ceremony, thus making things less confusing. Walking through all these minute details in advance, will reduce your stress and help to make your wedding ceremony run smoother. It is the easiest way to achieve wedding day peace of mind.

Most brides opt to have a rehearsal. Personally, I think the rehearsal is a great time to make sure everyone is on board with what their roles are and helps to clarify what they are supposed to do for the couple before, during, and after the ceremony. It is also a great time for everyone to meet each other if they have not already done so.

When I coordinate a wedding rehearsal, we always go through the highlights of the ceremony a minimum of two times and as many times necessary for everyone to be comfortable with what they are supposed to be doing. The first time is always

a mess – don't worry about that, each run through gets better. Usually twice is enough. And it's fun!

Who should attend the wedding rehearsal? All members of the wedding party including bride, groom, best man, maid of honor, bridesmaids, groomsmen, ushers, flower girl, ring bearer, readers, mothers and fathers, including the person you assigned to assist with lining everyone up. Although it's not required, ideally, the musician(s) or DJ will also attend so cues and timing can be coordinated. Everyone should arrive on time because we will need to start on time.

Who should be in charge of the rehearsal and ceremony? In my many years of officiating ceremonies, I have seen a lot of different ways to handle the rehearsal and ceremony. The best ones are when there is an event planner involved. I can tell you from experience that when the bride allows me to assist her, things go very well. When mom, caterer, or some other person tries to run things, confusion reigns. By the time a bride gets to her rehearsal, everyone in her family is tired of hearing about the wedding so an outside person, someone who is objective and separate from the family, can help to keep the chaos in check and get more done in the allotted time.

So, let's review what should take place, so rehearsal goes well and the ceremony is stress-free.

Most brides think the most important part of any ceremony is the walking in – the processional and the walking out – the recessional. But I have found people want to know what their role is supposed to be during the ceremony, so I advise each member of the bridal party about where they should stand, what order they are to process and recess in, and what role they have. So to start, let's review who is a part of the ceremony.

The best man and maid or matron of honor stand closest to the groom and the bride, respectively. Typically, the best man holds the rings while the matron or maid of honor holds the bride's bouquet during the exchange of vows and rings and helps her with her dress.

The groomsmen often act as ushers before the start of the ceremony, and one or two may escort the bride's mother, the groom's mother, and other special guests to their seats. They might also unroll the aisle runner if there is one.

The bridesmaids assist the bride to get dressed and help her, so she doesn't forget anything before the start of the ceremony.

The flower girl(s) typically toss flower petals or might carry a basket or flower ball, and the ring bearer carries a ring pillow, preferably *not* with the real rings. **Personally, I don't think a toddler should be in charge of the rings**, but you can add fake ones to the pillow. The flower girl(s) and ring bearer walk in just before the bride.

The father of the bride typically escorts his daughter down the aisle and will often say something about "giving her away," although it is not unusual for the mom to escort her daughter as well.

Sometimes the groom's parents will escort their son to the place of ceremony, too. So what exactly takes place at the rehearsal?

I like to remind people why they are here and what will happen, and if they concentrate, we can be done quicker. Rehearsal should only take about 20-30 minutes if everyone cooperates. I always tell everyone to be well hydrated at the ceremony, especially if the wedding will be outside and if the weather is expected to be hot. Don't lock your knees. Locking your knees can cause the blood flow to slow down, so keep your knees slightly bent and you will not pass out!

Choose how you want the men to hold their hands: in front or behind, but definitely not in their pockets! I usually suggest they mirror the groom. The women should stand up straight; elbows bent for a graceful appearance and bouquets at the belly-button level.

Ten Helpful Tips

Know in advance where any large decorative structures (wedding arch, ferns, pedestals, etc.) are going to be so we can figure out where we can and cannot stand to avoid those areas.

Have a few chairs set up to represent the front row so you can judge the amount of space needed for the aisle and to practice escorting and seating the mothers.

Many brides and bridesmaids bring mock bouquets made of paper plates and ribbon to the rehearsal. This is an excellent idea so everyone can get used to holding them. The bouquets look best held at belly-button level. The bride may also want to have a mock veil or train if she is going to wear them in the ceremony.

If there is going to be an aisle runner, decide ahead of time who will pull it out and at what point in the processional it will happen. Traditionally, it is done just before the bride's entrance, but I have seen it done many different ways including the entire wedding party walking on the runner. I don't recommend using a runner outside unless it is a very heavy fabric. Putting down an aisle runner must be done slowly, and the runner should be held low to the ground; otherwise, it will probably tear.

Decide how you want everyone lined up – not just for the processional but for their position in the ceremony area. Decide if you want the groomsmen to come in all together in the beginning or paired up with bridesmaids. If they are to enter in pairs, decide in advance who will walk with whom. Decide who walks in with the bride, if the person is going to say anything, and if this person will sit down immediately or stand for a few moments. This person needs to know what to do and what to say.

Assign people to do certain tasks. For example, who will hold the rings? (Please don't put them on the ring pillow.) You will need to designate someone to do this. Assign someone to hold the bride's bouquet during the ceremony. Assign someone to walk the bride and groom's mothers to their seats. Assign someone to bring

the license to the Officiant before the ceremony so s/he can check it for accuracy. Assign someone to set up the table for your special ritual, if applicable. Assign someone to assist with lining everyone up just before the ceremony.

If you are going to have a special ritual during the ceremony such as sand pouring, candle lighting, and other types of rituals, decide where you want the table for this special rite and discuss how this will be set up to accomplish the it smoothly and so your guests can see what you are doing.

The rehearsal time should be dedicated to rehearsing. Make sure everyone is available. Ask them to come at least 30 minutes early to ensure they arrive on time. A month's notice to the Officiant is appreciated.

If you choose not to have a rehearsal, use this list to coordinate things and inform your Officiant of the choices you have made, it will make things go smoother on the day of your ceremony.

Finally, one last note to the bride: Usually by the time you get to this point in your planning process, your friends and family have stopped listening to you. Consider someone else (ideally your Officiant) who does not know your family to

handle the rehearsal. This person can step in and provide the leadership necessary to accomplish the task of completing and getting through the rehearsal.

Congratulations and good luck with your rehearsal!

"Rites and Ceremony are necessary for people so they avoid physical injury."

Carl Jung

Your wedding day emergency kit should contain the following:

For the Bride:

- Brush or comb

- Hairspray or extra hair product, pins, etc.

- Dental floss

- Extra pantyhose if you're wearing them

- Tissues

- Mints

- Compact mirror

- Makeup essentials, such as blemish concealer, lip color, mascara, and foundation

- Perfume or scented spray

- Antacid and pain reliever

- Hand lotion

- A small sewing kit, which includes needles, thread, and safety pins

- A lint brush or you can add a roll of double-sided tape, which can come in handy for quick hem fixes and other potential emergencies

- Stain remover

- White chalk. If you get a spot or stain on your wedding dress, don't panic. Dab it over with chalk to mask it. Also, make sure to ask at the dress boutique or your seamstress what to do if you spill something on your dress. Should you get out the club soda or baby powder?

- Deodorant. It's a stressful day; smell your best.

- Tampons or pads

- Wet wipes

- Stain-removing wipes.

- Cell phones and important phone numbers

- Healthy, energy-boosting snacks, such as fruit and granola bars

- Chocolate. Women tend to get frazzled and stressed out on their wedding day. Chocolate helps!

For the Groom:

- Extra black socks
- Brush or comb
- Cologne
- Corsage pins
- Shirt buttons
- Lint brush or roller
- Small sewing kit with buttons, needles, safety pins, thread, and small scissors

- Shoe polish
- Breath mints
- Deodorant
- Extra tie

You can purchase pre-made wedding emergency kits, but it is just as easy, and much less expensive, to assemble your own.

Seven sensational ceremony ideas

Form a Bond with your Officiant – be honest, open, and allow him or her to learn about you as a couple.

Speak From the Heart – Your vows should reflect the magnitude of the commitment you are about to make. They should not be embarrassing or cryptic. You can write them yourself or select something pre-written that speaks to you.

Combine Cultures – Personalize your ceremony with elements from both your cultural backgrounds.

Plan Ahead – Select rituals that reflect who you are as a couple; be unique. Take the time to figure out how to make your ceremony different. You don't have to break a glass or light a candle; you can do something different.

Include Your Whole Crew – The ceremony is a great time to honor important family members and close friends who aren't in your wedding party. Maybe choose several short readings performed by special readers.

Stick to Your Guns – Do not let anyone tell you what you are doing is wrong. You need to be comfortable and happy with your choices; it is your wedding, after all! If what you want is possible, ask your Officiant to help you.

Have Fun! – It is OK to use humor in your wedding ceremony; just don't use crude language or embarrass anyone.

"Couples select ceremony music whether it is traditional, contemporary or eclectic that will reflect their style and taste and sets the tone for the entire event"

Event Entertainment

A mastiff and salmon sliders

As a wedding Officiant, I get the opportunity to work not only with interesting couples but also with lots of animals in my weddings. Couples in their search for something different, something authentic, something entertaining, will use animals to create some interest in their weddings. In most cases, the dog or cat is part of the couple's family and holds a special place in the hearts and minds of the couple.

I see dogs more than any other animal. Recently at a very upscale hotel, a huge 195-pound Mastiff was the best man, dressed to the nines with cuffs and tie. He behaved perfectly during the ceremony, although he thought the rose petals might be dog biscuits and had to check this out when the flower girl came down the aisle. This gorgeous animal scared a young lady carrying some salmon sliders during cocktail hour. He woofed at her, and the salmon sliders lived up to their name and slid everywhere! He just wanted one – after all, it was a cocktail hour!

Once there were two tiny Chihuahuas dressed like the bride and groom and carried in a basket by a bridesmaid; They were so cute! Then in June, there was a little Jack Russell dressed as the ring bearer in a sweater in 100-degree heat! Really! Poor little girl – she was better behaved than most of the bridal party! I just think the sweater in the heat was too much!

Sometimes I see a cat, but I think like our friend Grumpy Cat (otherwise known as Tardar Sauce), most cats are far too superior to participate in such an event; it would be beneath one's dignity. (Smirk!)

Another thing I see is the use of birds… especially the hawk who "delivers the rings." The hawk doesn't actually bring in the rings but gives the illusion that it

does, which makes it a pretty cool illusion. The best man pretends not to be able to find the rings; then he turns around and puts on a glove with a treat for the hawk. At the back of the audience, a licensed falconer releases the hawk. Then the hawk flies to the best man for the treat, ostensibly delivering the wedding rings. The Officiant removes the rings from the thumb of the best man and the hawk then flies back to the falconer. This really wows the guests; it is a great display of falconry and bravery.

Doves are also used as an impressive statement at the end of a wedding ceremony. When done correctly; this is so sweet. The doves are released by the couple or sometimes the entire bridal party. The doves simply fly back to the roost they came from; somehow they know where to go; Amazing, actually.

Other animals like horses are used to either pull a wagon or cart to bring the bride and then take the couple away from the ceremony site. Or the groom can ride in on a white horse like Prince Charming. In Indian weddings, sometimes an elephant brings the groom to the ceremony location.

Another interesting custom in India used to ward off bad spirits, is the marriage between human and animals. Although animal/human marriage are not officially recognized, they are still practiced in a few places.

So think about how you might include your animal friend in your ceremony. Your pet might be a unique and fun way to embrace something different for your wedding ceremony!

"Marriage is not a noun; it's a verb. It isn't something you get. It's something you do. It's the way you love your partner every day."

Angelis, Barbara De

Steamy, wet and frozen wedding ceremonies

Outside weddings here in the Mid-Atlantic region are so beautiful when the weather cooperates. But what happens when you don't have a backup plan? Will you get wet? Do you have a tent or indoor space set aside for the ceremony? Will

it be cold or super-hot? What about your guests and your grandparents; can you imagine them wet and cold or hot and sweltering?

Following are a few stories that may convince you to have a backup plan on your wedding day:

Rain in the Park Ceremony

The day started rainy. I don't mean sprinkles; I mean pouring. All day right up to and through the ceremony the rain came down. The ceremony was in a pretty

memorial garden. The couple wanted a beautiful candle-lighting ceremony, music from a boom box and, of course, to be a dry, well-dressed and elegant couple. Just before the ceremony start time, the guests arrived, they came carrying patio and beach umbrellas. Someone pulled out a roll of plastic sheeting from their trunk and with some help we created a relatively rain-free spot under several umbrellas and the plastic sheeting. The space created was just big enough for the couple and me. One of the guests had to kneel down behind me, (head literally at my bottom!) to hold the umbrella; no one had thought to bring the stands. My pants were wet from the knees down (Luckily I brought an extra pair for the wedding later in the day). Although the ceremony was beautiful and moving, guests stood under umbrellas, the candle wouldn't light, and the boom box didn't work, because it shorted out from getting so wet. After the ceremony, everyone retired to a local VFW. To my surprise, the couple spent 3-weeks remodeling the place. It was beautiful, Feng Shui design had been applied to the room and an amazing, beautiful space was created. Many of the guests commented on why we were out in the rain when the ceremony could have easily been in a dry space.

Steamy, Hot Ceremony

It was mid-July at a gorgeous, botanical garden with a ceremony scheduled for 2 PM; it was the height of the day, the temperature was 102, with 97% humidity. Baby, it was hot outside! The guests arrived on time, sat in the full sun; getting up after a few minutes to find a shady spot. I noticed there were several elderly people sitting and fanning themselves. I felt sorry for these people. There was no water on site, no drinks at all. One and a half hours later the couple and their entourage finally arrive. That's when the bottled water and soda's arrived. The ceremony was nearly an hour long, not something I usually do or recommend, but it was what they wanted. Following the ceremony, everyone retired to an air conditioned hall. The hall was beautiful! Why, oh why, didn't they get married there! We all would have been more comfortable! Most of us were exhausted from the heat. The air conditioning was such a relief!

Frozen Ceremony

The gorgeous waterfront venue is simply the best place to hold a wedding ceremony if, you want a water view, but not so much in November. Seriously, it was around 40 degrees outside but with the wind blowing, it felt more like 28 degrees. It was really cold! The bride wore a strapless dress. I had on a suit with long-johns underneath; I did my best to stay warm, only my hands and face were cold. There were two little flower girls around 4–5 years old. The bride insisted they remove their coats and the sweaters their moms had given them. These two little ones cried all the way down the aisle. The ceremony was around 20–25 minutes long; although I did talk fast, everyone was cold. Following the ceremony practically

everyone ran into the warmth of the lodge for the reception. Don't think my hands and face thawed out for at least 30 minutes. Everyone was searching for coffee and hot chocolate instead of cold beer!

So, if I have learned anything, no matter what time of year, using your backup plan is a safe option. Although each of the scenarios above make for a memorable moment, there is something to be said for keeping your guests and vendors comfortable too.

Really cool ritual ideas…

Are you and your partner nerds? Here is a perfect ritual for your wedding! A unity volcano. Personally, I haven't a clue, but you two are scientists, so you can put it together, and I will write some words to make it happen. Enjoy!

Ying-Yang

The Ying-yang ceremony is perfect if your colors are black and white. The yin-yang is very much like a marriage. Not only do the light and dark require the equal presence of the other for balance, they cannot exist without the other. For within each half, there is   a

small circle of the opposite color, a small circle which shows that nothing is absolute. In all yin, there is a bit of yang. And within all yang, there is a bit of yin. Each exists in the other, and each needs the other to exist.

Pinky Swear

The Pinky Swear or Promise is a when two people entwine their pin- ky fingers and make a promise to one another then kiss their thumbs and touch them together to seal the deal or promise. The pin-

ky swear signifies a promise that cannot be broken unless all parties agree to it. This swear is considered to be the highest promise of all promises, and the pinky would be severed if the promise is broken.

CELEBRATING THE FAMILY

Children

What a great way to include your children in the ceremony. Receiving an item is a symbolic way to include the children in the wedding and the relationship.

Native American Wedding Cup

This beautiful ritual is an easy and simple way to symbolize the joining together of two lives.

Binding with a Red Thread

An ancient legend states that a couple is united by an invisible red thread that continuous shrinks until the couple is united in marriage…

Ceremonial Labyrinth.

Walking the labyrinth is symbolic of the different places you both come from. A ceremonial labyrinth has two entrances and one exit. Now you will walk together for the remainder of your days on earth.

Handfasting

Handfasting a pagan ritual that comes to us from the Celts. It is where the term tying the knot comes from.

Espresso Ceremony

The sugar as it is stirred into the rich black liquid represents the sweetness of life; the joy and passion. The Cream represents the color of love as it takes away the bitterness and smooth's out the flavor and just like a good team, the sugar and cream are a perfect pair and make the coffee complete.

Advice from the pros

Photographer Kelly Hahn suggests keeping photos in mind when planning your hairstyle for the wedding day and especially during the ceremony. A long lock or bang across your face is very becoming but not if it is on the side that faces the guests and photographer. While we work to capture both faces of the couple from various sides, there are just some images best captured straight on, like the ring exchange and the kiss. On a windy day, if you have a long, flowing hairstyle, think about facing the wind, so that your hair is blowing back and away from your face, rather than across it.

Kelly Hahn Photography • 1-240-285-3677 • info@kellyhahnphotography.com

Long gone are the day of the "3-hour wedding package", today's couples have many options available to them – Limousines, Shuttle buses, Limo-buses and even sedans. Thinking outside of the box can help ease your transportation woes for you and your guests.

Are you getting married at a private home or small venue with no parking? Shuttle your guests from a community parking lot, church or school.

You want a limousine to get your there but what about the end of the day? You DO NOT have to rent a limousine for the entire time your celebration is going on, rent it for the beginning and have it return at the end.

Here are some tips to help you navigate this part of your special day:

Book Early: You should hire your transportation company about six months before your special day. If your wedding will fall in May,

June, September of October, the earlier is always better. It is understandable that you won't have exact information but you will have the basic information. Reputable limousine companies under- stand this and will work with you.

Transportation for your guests: If you have guests staying at ho- tels it helps to provide them with a ride from the hotel to the wed- ding and back. For this purpose, you can hire a charter or shuttle bus. If a hotel says it has a shuttle, just ask for a peck of the vehicle. You cannot transport 150 guests in a ten passenger van! If alcohol is being served, this option is always worth considering.

Make your reservation in person (if possible): Research the limou- sines rental companies online, phone them and meet them in per- son to make the final booking. Always ask to see the vehicle before booking. Always read reviews! The gamble to save a dollar or two doesn't necessarily work out in your favor!

Get a contract and detailed itinerary: So there is no stress on your day, tell your limousine company exactly what you want to be planned for your special day, any stops, the number of people, etc. Ask if you can bring food or drink with you. Most states make it illegal for limousine companies to provide alcohol, but they do allow the customer to provide it. Ask about any other special services. You should have a final conversation with your limousine company about a week before your wedding. Don't just give a credit card and hope for the best, this never works!

The best piece of advice we can give is to relax and enjoy your day!

ON THE TOWN Limousines, Inc.

www.onthetownlimousines.com

We love planning weddings, but that's because we're professionals. But for couples and sometimes family members, it can be a very stressful process. It is important the couple, and maybe the couple's family agree on a budget, the budget is a very important factor when planning your wedding. For example, you don't want to look at a venue that costs $7,000 when your total overall budget is $10,000.

Also, research, it's critical you research all your wedding professionals, ask plenty of questions and make sure they're the right professional for you! Hiring the right professionals for your special day and not family members is imperative, i.e. the uncle that's a DJ at the family reunions or the father who loves to take pictures.

Wedding professionals have an agreement and contract of services holding them liable for your day; wedding professionals have more vested because their business is on the line if something goes wrong on your wedding.

And last but definitely not least, it's important to remember not to get lost in the planning of a wedding, the most important people at the wedding is you – the bride and groom, the soon-to-be "Mr. & Mrs."

Tiffanie "EventPlanner" McCoy, Owner, Wedding/Event Planner
Bird of Paradise Events
www.birdofparadiseevents.com • weddings@birdofparadiseevents.com

Event Entertainment

410-429-4602

dave@eventdjs.com

www.djsmaryland.com

Kelly Hahn Photography

1-240-285-3677

info@kellyhahnphotography.com

www.ceremonyalchemy.com